Writing Mastery
Expository

EXPOSITORY ESSAY

WORKBOOK TWO

Copyright © 2019 by Munaii Bookworks

All rights reserved. This book or any portion thereof may not be reproduced or used in any manner whatsoever without the express written permission of the publisher except for the use of brief quotations in a book review.

Printed in the United States of America
First Printing, 2019

ISBN: 978-0-9861018-9-2

Munaii Bookworks
16192 Coastal Hwy, Lewes, DE 19958, USA

EXPOSITORY CONTENTS

Introduction 5
Prior Knowledge Expository 6
Expository Pre-assessment 7
Expository Checklist 8
Narrative vs Expository 10
Expository Essay Overview 13
Expository Question Analysis 14
Brainstorming 16
Expository Essay Plan 17
Hooks 18
Context 21
Thesis Statement 22
The Introduction 24
Body Paragraph 1 25
Body Paragraph (Idea 2) 26
Body Paragraph (Idea 3) 27
So What Conclusions 28
Conclusion Paragraph 29
Voice 30
First Draft 31

- Essay Checklist 33
- Revising Sentences 35
- Revising Sentences 36
- Anecdote 37
- Word Choices 38
- Editing 40
- Final Draft 41
- Tools 43
- Transition Words 44
- Completed Plans 45
- Body Paragraph (Idea 1) 47
- Body Paragraph (Idea 2) 48
- Body Paragraph (Idea 3) 49
- Conclusion 50
- Voice 51
- Final Essay 52
- Final Exam 54
- Resources 55

INTRODUCTION

Welcome to the Writing Mastery course: Expository writing. This is the second course in the Authorkid program and can be taken alone or in conjunction with the other courses offered.

By going through the online videos and following the directions in this book, you will be a master in this type of academic writing. Each section is explained and builds on each previous step. Examples are given as well as tools to help you become an accomplished writer.

Enjoy.

PRIOR KNOWLEDGE EXPOSITORY

Write down characteristics of expository writing in each space.

EXPOSITORY PRE-ASSESSMENT

Before you begin the course, write an expository essay to the best of your ability.

> "I believe the greatest gift you can give your family and the world is a healthy you." Joyce Meyer

Write an essay about the importance of good health.

EXPOSITORY CHECKLIST

Essay: Introductory Paragraph	Check if done	Date
	Date:	Check when completed
The opening paragraph must complete three tasks.		
1. Hook		
2. Context		
3. Thesis		
Essay: Body of 2 or more Paragraphs		
1. Each major point is discussed in its own paragraph.		
2. These paragraphs include:		
a. A topic sentence.		
b. at least three major support sentences.		
c. Explanation and analysis of evidence.		
d. A concluding sentence that transits to the next paragraph.		

Essay: Concluding Paragraph		
The ending of the essay must complete three tasks.		
1. Restate the three major points and the thesis.		
2. Give the readers at least one new point of information to think about (optional).		
3. So what conclusion and hook restatement.		
Other Craft details		
Figurative Language		
Sentence variety		
Voice		
Transitions		
Anecdote		
Effective word choice		

NARRATIVE VS EXPOSITORY

Narrative
- Tells a story
- Focuses on one moment
- Author's purpose is to entertain
- Reader's purpose is to be entertained

Expository
- Gives information
- Author gives reasons and examples to support the thoughts and information
- Author's purpose is to inform
- Reader learns and is informed.

Both follow the writing process

In your own words, write a paragraph to explain the differences between an expository text and a personal narrative text.

_____
_____
_____
_____

Important information

The same prompts can be used for both narrative and expository writing.
Prompt: Write about your favorite season.

Narrative example

Straightaway, I jumped out of the car and ran and ran towards the apple trees. Summer was gone. Outside the wind blew, sending pretty leaves to the ground. I could smell the cool air and the sweet apples ripening on the trees. More than the scent, was an amazing sight to behold in the distance. The whole world had turned a canvas of bold reds, oranges, and browns. I loved to see trees this color and as I walked towards my first apple tree. I picked a red apple and after rubbing it clean on my sweater, I took my first bite. Yum.

Expository example

Why do people even like winter? Why do they like summer? One is too cold and the other is too hot. Spring is just rain but fall? Now that's an awesome season. There is so much to love about Fall. The weather, apples, and colors. What's not to love about the weather. It's just perfect to take brisk walks and to take in the sights. The apple picking ranks high up there as my favorite activity and that usually happens in the fall. Don't forget the apple cider too. Finally, I absolutely love the colors. Have you seen anything so beautiful as trees blushing in red and laughing in orange and dancing in brown? Fall is the best season for me.

Write about:

Your favorite subject or favorite person

Narrative Paragraph

_____
_____
_____
_____
_____
_____
_____
_____

Expository Paragraph

_____
_____
_____
_____
_____
_____
_____
_____

EXPOSITORY ESSAY OVERVIEW

Each part of the essay will require a planning table.

Use any planning structure you are comfortable with.

PLAN

INTRODUCTION

It must have a hook, thesis and context

Can be 5-10 sentences

Expository essay

The effective expository essay has several essential components. It needs to be planned. The essay itself contains one introductory paragraph, 2-10 body paragraphs, and one concluding paragraph

CONCLUSION

Must have restated thesis, summary of ideas, so what idea and restated hook,

It can be 4-10 sentences.

BODY PARAGRAPHS

Must have transition words, evidence, explanation of evidence and transition to next paragraph.

This can be 5-10 sentences.

EXPOSITORY QUESTION ANALYSIS

PRE-WRITING

After reading the prompt, write an explanation of it using your own words.

READ the information in the box below.

> There are people in our lives who are special to us. Sometimes this person is a teacher or coach, a parent, a brother or sister, or even a friend.

THINK about the people you care about.
WRITE about one person who has been important to you. Explain what makes this person special.

Be sure to–

- **clearly state your central idea**
- **organize your writing**
- **develop your writing in detail**
- **choose your words carefully**

In your own words, write down what this essay prompt means. Try not to look back when you start writing.

BRAINSTORMING

PRE-WRITING

List all the Special people in your life.

SPECIAL PEOPLE

This is a great time to think of all the people who mean something to you. Think of family members, friends, and teachers.

Brainstorm.

EXPOSITORY ESSAY PLAN

There are many types of graphic organizers that can be used to plan an expository essay. Practice drawing your favorite organizer in a short amount of time.

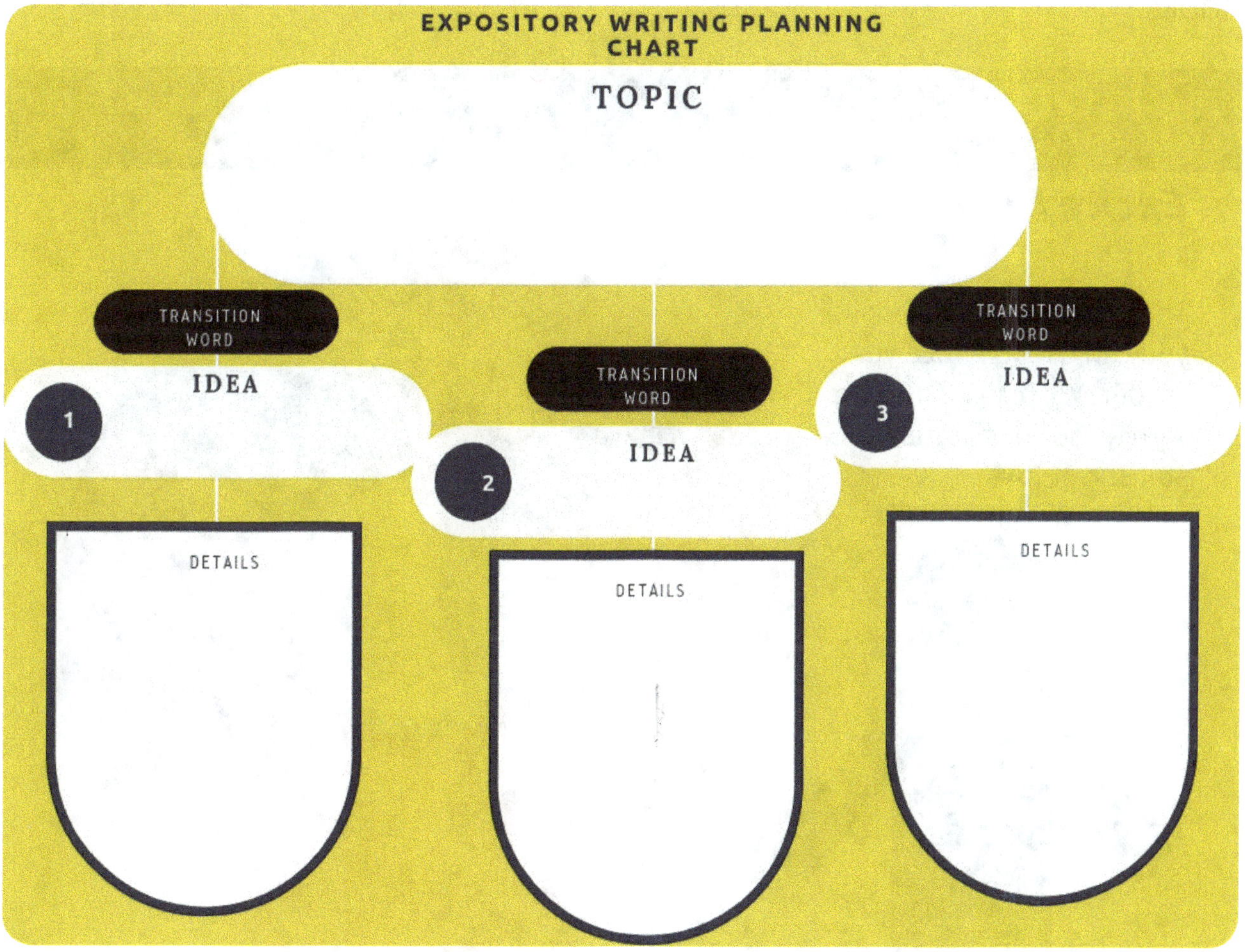

EXPOSITORY WRITING PLANNING CHART

TOPIC

TRANSITION WORD — IDEA 1 — DETAILS

TRANSITION WORD — IDEA 2 — DETAILS

TRANSITION WORD — IDEA 3 — DETAILS

HOOKS

Hooks excite the reader.

Make sure your essay begins in an engaging way by using one of the following hooks.

Hooks

Excite the Reader

These are just some hooks you can use to entice your reader. You can also begin with a shocking statement, statistic or joke.

- DIALOGUE
- QUESTION
- FAMOUS QUOTE
- ACTION
- ONOMOTAPOEA
- VIVID DESCRIPTION

Hooks Practice

Write a hook using all the different types you know.

Type of Hook	Example

Famous Quotes as Hooks

Find quotes on the following. Choose your own topics to find quotes on and complete the whole table.

Theme	Quote
education	"The more that you read, the more things you will know, the more that you learn, the more places you'll go."
Culture	
health	

CONTEXT

Context explains the topic to the reader before you give your opinion or ideas. Why do you need to include context? If you are writing an essay explaining how wonderful your school is, it helps the reader if you give the reader background information about the school. Where is it located? What's the building like? Then you can go into the reasons why it's so fantastic. Context is there to help the reader understand your essay and learn more from the facts you will be providing.

| technology | Video games | sports | music | Fast food |

Pick two topics from the list and write a hook and context about the <u>dangers</u> of each.

Topic	Hook and context

THESIS STATEMENT

A thesis statement answers the question, "What is your essay about?"

Tell the reader what your essay will be about in one sentence. Then answer the question, what is your essay about?

Here are some statements.

THESIS STATEMENTS

SET 1
- The health benefits of eating fruits and vegetables include clear thinking, better immune system, and healthy heart.
- Children should avoid using technology because of many dangers with radiation, addiction and lack exercise.
- It's interesting how music is powerful by helping autistic children, developing math understanding and in calming down babies.

SET 2
- You should eat fruit every day, for breakfast lunch and dinner and also for snack.
- Computers are very bad for you for many reasons when you use them all the time.
- You should do your research before making medical decisions by going online and asking friends and family about your ailments.

What do you notice about the 2 sets? Write your response here

_____

THESIS STATEMENT continued...

Almost all assignments, no matter how complicated, can be reduced to a single question. Your first step, then, is to condense the assignment into a specific question. For example:

Topic: Write a report to the local school board explaining the potential benefits of using computers in a fourth-grade class
Question: What are the potential benefits of using computers in a fourth-grade class?
Thesis: The potential benefits of using computers in a fourth-grade class are . . .

Strong OR WEAK THESIS

Weak: Eating fast food is bad and should be avoided.
Strong: Americans should eliminate the regular consumption of fast food because the fast food diet leads to preventable and expensive health issues, such as diabetes, obesity, and heart disease.

Weak: Humans should relocate to Mars
Strong:

Weak: Our School Is Too Dependent on Technology
Strong:

THE INTRODUCTION

Your introduction can be 3 sentences or more. Write one or two sentences for the hook, context, and thesis.

PARAGRAPH 1		
Each sentence in paragraph one is planned.		
HOOK	CONTEXT	THESIS STATEMENT
Begin your essay with an exciting beginning that hooks the reader.	Provide information the reader will need to understand the topic.	Set your thesis, your arguable position on the topic. What side will you take? What will you prove in your paper? What are you going to explore?

BODY PARAGRAPH 1

WRITE THE TOPIC SENTENCE THAT STATES THE MAIN IDEA

WRITE DOWN SPECIFIC EVIDENCE TO SUPPORT YOUR THESIS

ANALYZE YOUR EVIDENCE AND TELL THE READER WHAT IS IMPORTANT ABOUT YOUR EVIDENCE.

WRITE THE TRANSITION SENTENCE

BODY PARAGRAPH (IDEA 2)

WRITE THE TOPIC SENTENCE THAT STATES THE MAIN IDEA

WRITE DOWN SPECIFIC EVIDENCE TO SUPPORT YOUR THESIS

ANALYZE YOUR EVIDENCE AND TELL THE READER WHAT IS IMPORTANT ABOUT YOUR EVIDENCE.

WRITE THE TRANSITION SENTENCE

BODY PARAGRAPH (IDEA 3)

WRITE THE TOPIC SENTENCE THAT STATES THE MAIN IDEA	
WRITE DOWN SPECIFIC EVIDENCE TO SUPPORT YOUR THESIS	
ANALYZE YOUR EVIDENCE AND TELL THE READER WHAT IS IMPORTANT ABOUT YOUR EVIDENCE.	
WRITE THE TRANSITION SENTENCE	

SO WHAT CONCLUSIONS

SO WHAT

- *Is an imaginary dialogue with a friend about your topic.*
- *They ask your questions that will help deepen your thinking.*
- *After you restate you thesis and ideas they will ask. So what?*
- *After you answer so what they will ask "Why should anybody care"*
- *By answering these questions you take your conclusion to another level.*

So What Conclusion

You: Spending time in Disney, especially the moment on the magic carpet ride was a day I will never forget.

Friend: So what?

You: Well, It's important to spend time with family and being on the awesome ride.

Friend: Why sould anybody care?

You: Being with family and having such an experience is important because it makes us closer and builds lasting memories that we will look back on when we are also adults and have our own children.

CONCLUSION PARAGRAPH

1 OR 2 SENTENCES **TRANSITION AND RESTATE THESIS**	
3 OR 4 SENTENCES **SUMMARISE YOUR IDEAS**	
ANSWER SO WHAT? WHY SHOULD ANYBODY CARE? **3 OR 4 SENTENCES**	
2 OR 3 SENTENCES **CONNECT IT TO YOUR HOOK AND PUT IT ALL TOGETHER.**	

VOICE

As you put your essay together, consider your VOICE.

An expository essay doesn't have to be dry or boring. Your 'voice" or personality still needs to shine through the information you are delivering.

VOICE

Tone: How do you feel about the subject you are writing.
Topic: Dogs

Serious tone	Funny tone

FIRST DRAFT

Topic _____ Date _____

ESSAY CHECKLIST

Analyze your first draft use the check list

Essay: Introductory Paragraph	Check if done	Date
	Date:	Check when completed
The opening paragraph must complete three tasks.		
1. Hook		
2. Context		
3. State the thesis, the main idea of the paper.		
Essay: Body of Three Paragraphs		
1. Each major point is discussed in its own paragraph.		
2. These paragraphs include:		
a. a topic sentence.		
b. at least three major support sentences.		
Explanation and analysis of evidence.		

c. a concluding sentence that transits to the next paragraph.		
Essay: Concluding Paragraph		
The ending of the essay must complete three tasks.		
1. Restate the three major points and the thesis.		
2. Give the readers at least one new point of information to think about (optional).		
3. So what conclusion and hook restatement.		
Other Craft details		
Figurative Language		
Sentence variety		
Vocabulary		
Transitions		
Anecdote		

REVISING SENTENCES

Creating complex sentences

Look through your essay and find some sentences that can be revised. Create complex sentences by having two or more clauses joined by subordinating conjunction.

COMPLEX SENTENCES

SUBORDINATING CONJUCTIONS	OWN SENTENCES
while	While my friends were out playing on the beach, I practiced piano. *(subordinator — subjects — predicate)*
after	
although	
as	
because	
even if	
if	
lest	
now that	
since	
than	
though	
unless	
until, when	

REVISING SENTENCES

Revising Sentences with figurative Language

Sensory language adds color to your writing and adds your personality and unique way of thinking.

Figurative Language

**SIMILES, ALLITERATION, IDIOMS, AND CLICHES.
HERE ARE A FEW MORE TO TRY OUT. WRITE OUT YOUR OWN EXAMPLES.**

METAPHOR	comparing two unlike objects without using like or as.	My classroom was a circus after the exams.
PERSONIFICATION	Giving human characteristics to objects e.g the sun smiled.	
OXYMORON	two terms appear to contradict each other e.g deafening silence	
ALLUSION	Allusion is a brief and indirect reference to a person, place, thing or idea of historical, cultural, literary or political significance	I wasn't exactly Michael, but my free throws were not bad.

ANECDOTE

In some cases, it's a great idea to add an anecdote to your expository essay. An anecdote tells a small story to explain one of the ideas in your essay. It adds more interest and emphasizes the point. Anecdotes can work at the beginning or middle of the essay.

Write anecdotes to explain the following.

Topic	Anecdote
Safety	
Caring for pets	
Making new friends	
Sacrifice	
Taking care of your health	

WORD CHOICES

WORD CHOICES

said is still good	ALTERNATIVE WORDS
said	wondered, groaned, chided, whispered, declared
nice	
beautiful	
cold	
dirty	
walk	
run	
good	
scary	
happy	
angry	
hungry	
special	
strange	
asked	
hot	
enjoy	

Create sentences using your alternative word choices.

Word choice Practice

Write about a person, place or thing. Use colorful words and some figurative language.

Word: Giraffe
As tall as the trees moving through the forest above everyone. Shimmering golds and browns on soft furry skin. A neck as gracefully elongated like a ballerina and keen eyes intelligent and gentle. Floating through the forest, bending low to say hello

Practice: Pick your own word and describe it. Practice 5 more in your journal.

Word:

Word choice

Find 3-5 better word choices. Write them in the space.

big	good	nice	bad	happy
nice	pretty	walked	ran	like
scared	little	fast	mad	funny

EDITING

> How many mistakes can you find?
> Rewrite correctly.

Edit

Everybody has heard the saying that Winners never quite and quitters never win. Despite all that still many people will quit before the day is over, Not giving up when the road gets tough, and the obstacles mount is not difficult. There are ways you can ensure your reach you goal. You have to remember why you started in the first place, You must get support and you definitely have to visualize the end goal.

Add capitalization, commas, quotation marks etc.

FINAL DRAFT

Final Draft Topic _____ Date _____

_____
_____
_____
_____
_____
_____
_____
_____
_____
_____
_____
_____
_____
_____
_____
_____

TOOLS

TRANSITION WORDS

Transition words

		EXAMPLES
TIME AND SEQUENCE	first, second, finally, in conclusion, in summary, meanwhile	First, I know that the teacher saw the tests.
GIVING EXAMPLES	for example, in particular,	Food can be heal you or kill you. For instance, too much sugar can result in deadly diseases.
ADDING INFORMATION	moreover, also, and	Eating healthy is good for you. Moreover, it can be fun and delicious.
RESULT OR SIMILARITY	as a result, consequently, therefore, likewise, similarly	Moana wrote the best essay. therefore she won the trophy.

Write your own sentences using the 4 different types of transitions listed above.

COMPLETED PLANS

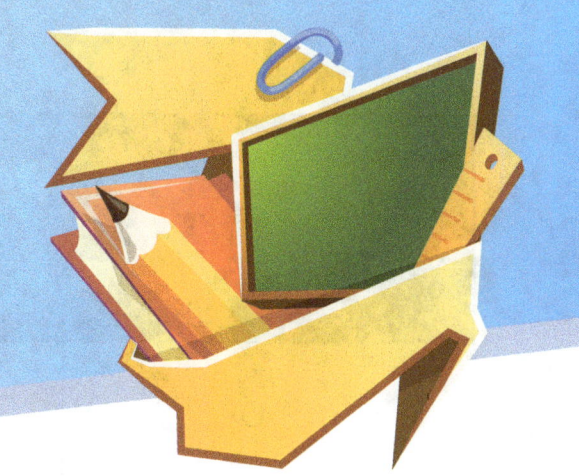

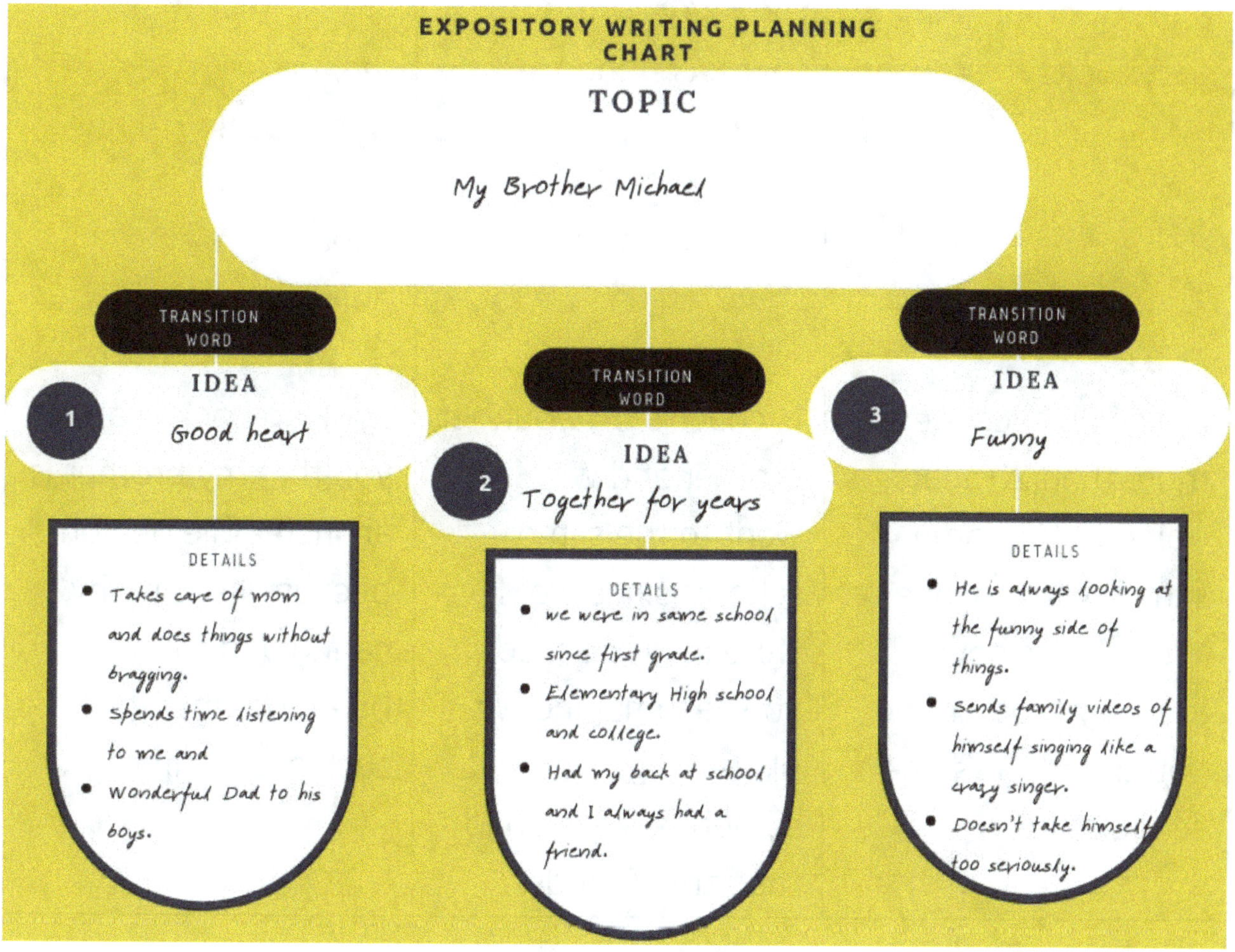
EXPOSITORY WRITING PLANNING CHART
TOPIC
My Brother Michael
TRANSITION WORD
1
IDEA
Good heart
DETAILS
• Takes care of mom and does things without bragging.
• spends time listening to me and
• Wonderful Dad to his boys.
TRANSITION WORD
2
IDEA
Together for years
DETAILS
• we were in same school since first grade.
• Elementary High school and college.
• Had my back at school and I always had a friend.
TRANSITION WORD
3
IDEA
Funny
DETAILS
• He is always looking at the funny side of things.
• Sends family videos of himself singing like a crazy singer.
• Doesn't take himself too seriously.

PARAGRAPH 1

Each sentence in paragraph one is planned.

HOOK	CONTEXT	THESIS STATEMENT
Begin your essay with an exciting beginning that hooks the reader.	Provide information the reader will need to understand the topic.	Set your thesis, your arguable position on the topic. What side will you take? What will you prove in your paper? What are you going to explore?
Have you ever spent more than 20 years going to the same school with anyone? Well, that is how long my brother and I attended the same schools.	Michael is my younger brother and we went to the same schools since we were in grade 1. So you can imagine we played together and sometimes even had the same friends.	Looking back I can tell you that my brother is an incredible person because he is funny, caring and we have been together for such a long time.

BODY PARAGRAPH (IDEA 1)

WRITE THE TOPIC SENTENCE THAT STATES THE MAIN IDEA	Most people tend to fight with their siblings whereas my brother and I have actually spent so many years together in the same schools and we rarely fought.
WRITE DOWN SPECIFIC EVIDENCE TO SUPPORT YOUR THESIS	What makes my brother special is that we went to elementary school, high school and college together. I remember in elementary he used to protect me from bullies and I always watched over him. In College it was wonderful having him there because we were so far from home.
ANALYZE YOUR EVIDENCE AND TELL THE READER WHAT IS IMPORTANT ABOUT YOUR EVIDENCE.	It seems that my brother, Michael knows me more than anyone else in my family because he was there when I was little all the way to graduating college on the same day. This has definitely made us closer.
WRITE THE TRANSITION SENTENCE	Besides spending so much time together, there are so many more amazing qualities that my brother has.

BODY PARAGRAPH (IDEA 2)

WRITE THE TOPIC SENTENCE THAT STATES THE MAIN IDEA	When we were little, we used to ride bikes to school. I remember one day our friends were late for school and my brother. Mike carried the friend on his bike. He has such a caring and good heart.
WRITE DOWN SPECIFIC EVIDENCE TO SUPPORT YOUR THESIS	What makes him an exceptional human being is how kind he is. Even as an adult, he is always caring for others, opening his home to family and giving people what they need to succeed in life.
ANALYZE YOUR EVIDENCE AND TELL THE READER WHAT IS IMPORTANT ABOUT YOUR EVIDENCE.	Having a great heart and being generous is so important because what goes around comes aroung. We all love and respect him and I know that the good he gives out, will come back to him.
WRITE THE TRANSITION SENTENCE	So what's the point of being kindhearted and not having a sense of humor? I think you need both.

BODY PARAGRAPH (IDEA 3)

WRITE THE TOPIC SENTENCE THAT STATES THE MAIN IDEA	My brother is always laughing, enjoying life, laughing at himself and laughing with others. Did I say laughing 3 times? Yes, because there is no dull moment with him.
WRITE DOWN SPECIFIC EVIDENCE TO SUPPORT YOUR THESIS	Having a sense of humor definitely makes my brother, Mike, a remarkable human being. Even in dire moments, he tends to want to find the funny side.
ANALYZE YOUR EVIDENCE AND TELL THE READER WHAT IS IMPORTANT ABOUT YOUR EVIDENCE.	Why is it important to have a sense of humor? Well, for one you don't take yourself seriously and people enjoy being around people who laugh and ejnoy life, even when things are tough.
WRITE THE TRANSITION SENTENCE	All this shows me that I am a lucky person to have a brother who embodies all these characteristics.

CONCLUSION

1 OR 2 SENTENCES **TRANSITION AND RESTATE THESIS**	Even though there are many special people in my lige I chose to write about my brother Mike because I love his heart, his sense of humor and the fact that we spent so many years together in the same schools.
3 OR 4 SENTENCES **SUMMARISE YOUR IDEAS**	Spending time with him as a kid, an adolescent and an adult has definitely brought us closer. Moreover, I got to enjoy his sense of humor for years and watch his kind heartedness up close.
ANSWER SO WHAT? WHY SHOULD ANYBODY CARE? **3 OR 4 SENTENCES**	Not many people spend that much time together with someone, that they know each other so well and are there for each other without getting on each others nerves. I can say that I have a brother who is also a friend and that is rare.
2 OR 3 SENTENCES **CONNECT IT TO YOUR HOOK AND PUT IT ALL TOGETHER.**	It would seem that our parents putting us in the same schools has definitely created a bond that is sure to last a lifetime. Now our kids get to enjoy the same relationships.

VOICE

Topic: Fast Food

Serious tone	Funny tone
Do you really know what you are eating? Most of us never question what we pick up at the fast food chain restaurants that are at every corner. Several years ago, videos were released to reveal how chicken nuggets were made for Wendy's. Inexplicable, mixture of chemicals and unidentified meat were mashed together to create this long sticky, suspicious glue like substance. That is what children eat on a regular basis.	"I want McDonalds" is the cry in every house, heard across America. Why do we love fast food? Is it really that fast? It does make us put on weight very quickly. All those smells are chemically produced and our children can't wait to grab the toys that come with the packaging. The lines for this 'food' goes around blocks and blocks and in seconds the food is eaten in a car or even while walking. And we put on weight quickly and getting addicted to the sugar and fat in these foods rather quickly too. Yes, it is fast food. Fast way to die.

FINAL ESSAY

My Brother, My Friend

Introduction

Have you ever spent more than 20 years going to the same school with anyone? Well, that is how long my brother and I attended the same schools. Michael is 2 years younger than me and we went to the same school since we were in grade 1. So, you can imagine we played together at school, at home and often shared the same friends and hobbies. Looking back, I can tell you that my brother is an incredible person because he is funnier than a clown, caring and we have been together for most of our young lives.

Paragraph 2

Most people tend to fight with their siblings, but my brother and I have actually spent many years together in the same schools and we rarely fought, except when we were 7 and 9 and wanted this silly toy, but that's beside the point. What makes my brother special is that we went to elementary, high school, and University together. I remember in elementary he used to protect me from bullies and I always watched over him. In University, it was wonderful having him there because we were so far from home. It seems that my brother knows me more than anyone else in my family because he was there when I was little all the way to graduating college on the same day. This definitely made us closer and I always take his side even when he is being fooling. Besides spending so much time together, there are some amazing qualities that my brother has.

Paragraph 3

When we were little we used to ride bikes to school. I remember one day our friends were late for school and my brother Mike carried the friend on his bike. He has such a caring heart. What makes him an exceptional human being is how kind he is. Even as an adult, he is always caring for others, opening his home to family and giving what they need to succeed in life. Having a great heart and being generous is so important because what goes around comes around. We all love and respect him and I know that the good he gives out will come back to him.

Paragraph 4

My brother is always laughing, enjoying life, laughing at himself and laughing with others. Having a sense of humor definitely makes my brother, Mike, a remarkable human being. Why is it important to have a sense of humor? Well, for one you don't take yourself seriously and people enjoy being around people who laugh and enjoy life, even when things are tough. All this shows me that I am a lucky person to have a brother who embodies all these characteristics.

Conclusion

Even though there are many special people in my life I chose to write about my brother Mike because I love his heart, his sense of humor and the fact that we spent so many years together in the same schools. Spending time with him as a kid, an adolescent and an adult has definitely brought us closer. Moreover, I got to enjoy his sense of humor for years and watch his kind heartedness up close. Not many people spend time together with someone, that they know each other so well and are there for each other. I can say that I have a brother who is also a friend and that is rare. t would seem that our parents putting in the same schools has definitely created a bond that is sure to last a lifetime.

FINAL EXAM

READ the information in the box below.

> "None of us alone can save the nation or the world. But each of us can make a positive difference if we commit ourselves to do so."
> —**Cornel West**

THINK about ways you can make the world or your community better.

WRITE about ways that you can improve the world. Explain the ways that can make your world or community a better place to live.

Be sure to–

- **clearly state your central idea**
- **organize your writing**
- **develop your writing in detail**
- **choose your words carefully**

In your own words, write down what this essay question means. Try not to look back when you start writing.

_____

_____

_____

RESOURCES

https://writingcenter.unc.edu/tips-and-tools/conclusions/

https://writingcenter.fas.harvard.edu/pages/ending-essay-conclusions

https://literarydevices.net/figurative-language/

https://www.empoweringwriters.com/toolbox/teaching-voice-in-writing-barbara-mariconda/

https://tea.texas.gov/student.assessment/staar/writing/

www.ingramcontent.com/pod-product-compliance
Lightning Source LLC
Chambersburg PA
CBHW080833010526
44112CB00015B/2507